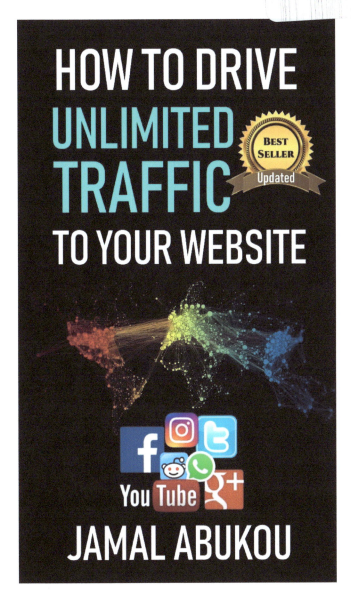

HOW TO DRIVE UNLIMITED TRAFFIC TO YOUR WEBSITE

BEST SELLER Updated

JAMAL ABUKOU

Why I Wrote This Book

I wrote this book because many people think that to make money one simply needs to build a website and customers will visit his/her website.

While building a website is surely needed, a key factor to the success of your website is driving traffic to it. It all comes down to this simple fact: "No Traffic, No Business".

So I wrote this book to help you discover so many ways to not only drive traffic to your website, but also to drive Unlimited Traffic. The good news is that most of these strategies will not cost you a single dollar.

Why You Should Read This Book

This book explores the fundamental strategies behind driving solid unlimited traffic to your website.

No matter what your website is and how hard you try to present its values to your customers, if you don't drive traffic to it the right way, you will struggle hard to make a business. It's really that simple. Visitors will not find you. You have to find them and drive them to your website.

Driving Traffic isn't a "Good Luck Guess". There is a strategy building behind Driving Traffic. Not a Rocket Science. Once you familiarize your self with the fundamentals behind these strategies, you're set to go.

Disclaimer

No part of this book may be reproduced in any form or by any electronic or mechanical means including information storage and retrieval systems, without permission in writing from the author. The only exception is by a reviewer, who may quote short excerpts in a review.

Although the author have made every effort to ensure that the information in this book was correct at press time, the author does not assume and hereby disclaim any liability to any party for any loss, damage, or disruption caused by errors or omissions, whether such errors or omissions result from negligence, accident, or any other cause.

This book is designed to provide information on how to drive unlimited traffic to your website only. This information is provided and sold with the knowledge that the author does not offer any legal or other professional advice. In the case of a need for any such expertise, consult with the appropriate professional. This book does not contain all information available on the subject.

This book has not been created to be specific to any individual's or organizations' situation or needs. Every effort has been made to make this book as accurate as possible. However, there may be typographical and or content errors. Therefore, this book should serve only as a general guide and not as the ultimate source of subject information. This book contains information that might be dated and is intended only to educate and entertain.

The author shall have no liability or responsibility to any person or entity regarding any loss or damage incurred, or alleged to have incurred, directly or indirectly, by the information contained in this book. You hereby agree to be bound by this disclaimer.

TABLE OF CONTENTS

Building Traffic Tributaries

The World Wide Web can be seen as a colossal sea of movement that is simply sitting tight to be tapped for your online business. The movement as of now exists, either on other individuals' destinations or through online associations, that are connected to terminals that go specifically into a man's home or office.

In this regard, you don't need to make activity; you need to figure out how to assemble tributaries that lead from that expansive sea back to your online contributions so existing movement has the chance to stream back to you. The channel that conveys this activity from the sea to your tributary is the various backlinks that you post everywhere throughout the Internet in different spots.

It's these connections that will bring activity from one zone of the WWW to your business site.

THE INDIVIDUAL AS A DROP OF WATER

Making this illustration a stride further, every person who is looking through the Internet can be seen as a drop of water that has the ability to spill out of one territory of the Internet to another. On the off chance that you additionally consider the conduct of every person, as well as the manner in which the water is appropriated on the Internet, you will find that individuals assemble in different territories, and a few spots are not intended to hold movement, but rather to circulate it considerably more, similar to web indexes.

At last, an internet searcher will list results from an inquiry that is finished utilizing an arrangement of watchwords, and in view of that outcome, the drop of water or individual ordinarily picks a couple of spots to jump to straightaway. That is one way that water is moved over the system of tributaries on the Internet.

The other way is proficient when the power of gravity itself pushes water starting with one territory then onto the next. On the Internet, this happens when such a large number of individuals discover something of significant worth that they begin posting increasingly backlinks back to a similar zone.

At the point when that occurs, the notoriety of the Web page increments and more water or individuals stream back to the website on the quality of mass introduction alone. We will investigate these two components inside and out to demonstrate to you best practices to get more movement to your site.

PAY SOMEONE TO BUILD A TRIBUTARY

Finally, another way that isn't as normal as the two different ways specified above is to pay somebody to come in and burrow a tributary, or huge amounts of connections back to your site. On the off chance that you do this through advertising systems like subsidiary and referral programs, it's viewed as alright.

On the off chance that you do this through spamming and compulsion, you'll wind up getting into lawful inconvenience. Note that when you are attempting to stand out enough to be noticed to your site, what you do needs to fall between great, legitimate conduct. Cybersquatting on another person's trademark name as your space name to get activity, for example, might be feasible, however it will cause you harm and ought to be stayed away from.

Directed Traffic

The Internet as a nebulous sea of movement is an awesome method to comprehend the elements of activity stream. This system of conduits has just been exceptionally created at times, with a few people as of now encountering awesome activity stream on their locales.

This is imperative to know since you would prefer truly not to simply put a delta beside a shapeless sea and drive huge amounts of untargeted movement back to your site. Every one of those drops may speak to a man who is on the web, however would they say they are the sort of individual who will purchase your items and administrations? Clearly not!

There is significantly more to building activity to your site than just numbers. It must be quality, directed activity that stands a decent possibility of making deals changes.

TARGET TRAFFIC RELATIVE TO YOUR NICHE

Regardless of whether you're getting activity from a web index or from some other website, your backlinks ought to appear in zones where the specialty is like your market portion. You would prefer not to offer gems and posting backlinks on pet locales or including catchphrases for pets.

That would just get movement that isn't keen on purchasing your items in any case. With a specific end goal to get superb movement that needs to get, you need to initially endeavor beyond any doubt that your endeavors are being put in the correct statistic.

THE LARGER THE POND, THE BETTER THE EXPOSURE

You need your specialty to be something that isn't narrow to the point that few individuals will be occupied with it, yet not be broad to the point that you won't characterize your statistic all around ok to target it either.

On the off chance that you find that the catchphrases that you are utilizing to create activity from web crawlers has a low inquiry volume, this shows with respect to different specialties, it most likely is a littler lake of water. It is smarter to distinguish a specialty that has some inalienable quality in numbers before you really begin to showcase it on the web.

When you locate a prevalent niche, you will likewise discover numerous other individuals advertising to that niche. The best specialties are those that have a high pursuit volume and a low focused factor, yet even exceedingly aggressive specialties can be accustomed to convey activity to your site.

You can target high activity puts around the WWW that are examining your specialty to add backlinks back to your site. These can incorporate prominent sites, discourse gatherings, sites that permit remarking, news stories, and online articles. The more activity that a site has effectively settled in your specialty, the more probable that you can redirect that movement back to your own endeavors by posting backlinks in those regions.

Notwithstanding for long range interpersonal communication locales that have extensive quantities of individuals visiting day by day, you need to focus on the movement to your specialty as opposed to aimlessly market to everybody and anybody.

Construct It Well

Before we go into the numerous territories with high movement that can be used to take individuals back to your site, we should talk about the instrument of the backlink in more detail. This will be the string of content that will be accustomed to bring individuals from one region of the WWW back to your site.

Consequently, you need to make certain that you fabricate these backlinks in the most ideal path conceivable, to draw in individuals who may read, as well as to stand out enough to be noticed as well.

THE BACKLINK

A backlink is a bit of HTML that is installed in other content and that is for the most part featured by means of an alternate content shading and bolding. It utilizes a stay content organization that in its most straightforward shape is this way:

```
<a
href="http://www.myurl.com">Myanchortext</a
>
```

What appears to a man perusing your backlink is the content that is composed in the "Myanchortext" territory. The genuine URL that you point to isn't saw, just the stay content. This is critical to recall with the goal that you fabricate your connections in a way that isn't just intriguing to your perusers, however that is likewise web index inviting as well.

Along these lines, you twofold your odds of getting movement, not simply from guests who are visiting that page, yet additionally from web indexes that are dissecting the stay content of these connections for content.

MAKE THEM INTERESTING TO BOTH!

One of the greatest oversights individuals make while adding backlinks to high movement territories is that they don't focus on the points of interest of the connection. Rather, you will see inadequately assembled joins that say, "Snap this," as their grapple content.

Truly, is that a solicitation to either a man or a web crawler that will catch either one's eye?! No! You need to take the view that you just have one opportunity to get that individual or web index's consideration, and that will be done through the nature of your backlink. Make the most of it.

Endeavor to utilize catchphrases that you've investigated in your grapple content to catch the internet searcher's eye. In any case, don't simply abandon it at that. Additionally, endeavor to influence the duplicate as fascinating to a guest as you to can so he/she actually feels constrained to click your backlink and be coordinated back to your site.

You can do this by adding quality remarks identified with your specialty in different regions and afterward enlightening individuals regarding some spectacular offer or data that is on your site as opposed to welcoming them to click. Explain to your peruser why he/she should tap on that connection; don't simply ask him/her to do it!

It's All About Marketing

At first, you will have a little inconvenience making sense of what is working and what isn't. Therefore, it's a smart thought to track the consequences of your backlinks so you can adjust how you present them in light of the outcomes you get. That implies that when you embed a backlink into a high movement region, you need to get a smart thought of how it is working.

How well did your duplicate draw in individuals to navigate to your site? Indeed, even in email showcasing, you need to know not exactly what number of individuals have opened your messages, however what number of have clicked back to your site when they read the duplicate.

This will give you a smart thought about what is most alluring to your gathering of people and what will assist you with building duplicate that nearly appears as though you're perusing their psyches.

Utilize A URL SHORTENER OR ANALYTIC PROGRAM

There are different devices you can use to check the activity levels returning to your site by means of your control board. They will even demonstrate the alluding site to you. The issue is that you need to be much more particular than that. You need to see which connections and advertising duplicate are more successful than the others.

For that, you need to track activity by each connection. You can do this by utilizing a URL shortener, or you can purchase an administration like AWeber.com for email promoting that offers an explanatory program to track interface navigate rates.

When you are first beginning, take a stab at utilizing a free URL shortener, similar to http://bit.ly, to track what number of individuals are tapping on your connections without paying anything. It'll enable you to become acclimated to following connections and what's in store when you post a connection.

PLAN YOUR MARKETING STRATEGY

Next, you'll need to set up connects to different advancements and contributions and set up an advertising technique for various locales around the WWW to produce presentation for those contributions.

For example, say you are advertising a digital book. You've concluded that you need to showcase it on Facebook, Twitter, and a few online journals. You set up the abbreviated URL, and after that you think about a few intriguing approaches to outline your connection to draw in consideration.

Make distinctive varieties utilizing watchwords in your stay content, yet utilize your abbreviated connection. After, you've conceptualized a few forms, you should need to utilize one form on Facebook, an alternate form on Twitter, and an alternate one on web journals.

You send an announcement to Facebook utilizing one form, a notice to Twitter by means of another, et cetera. You look into the outcomes and see which form was the most appealing.

You will discover as you do this an ever-increasing number of that some fascinating examples will show up with the destinations themselves, as well as with the socioeconomics that you are attempting to use.

You may find that a connection you believe is amazing gets not very many hits, while another that appeared to be to some degree unclear gets the most hits. There are a couple of factors that can influence this, and when you are very brave, do some investigation.

Timing Traffic

Before you go faulting or crediting the duplicate and the catchphrases, you need to consider that movement is anything but a steady on any site. Much the same as the sea has tides, the WWW has activity tides that travel every which way at various occasions of days, contingent upon the specialty and the statistic.

You must make sense of when the ideal time to present is on get the most movement. This is genuine whether you're attempting to catch the most eye for an eBay deal or whether you simply need to get the most movement from a site back to your site. Timing isn't the main variable that can influence your movement measurements, however it is the most persuasive.

At the point when IS EVERYONE ONLINE MOST?

The key inquiry you need to ask yourself when you plan on posting is, "When are individuals well on the way to be online to see your posting?" You remain to get significantly more movement when there are more individuals online just by working the chances.

It makes sense then that you need to know when individuals are most dynamic on various locales and plan your postings in like manner for the best execution.

It can change by statistic as well. On the off chance that your statistic is contained individuals who work days and are up during the evening, at that point your activity will appear during the evening.

On the off chance that your movement is generally originating from an unexpected nation in comparison to where you live, it bodes well to post on their hours and not all alone. Focus on your site activity logs from your current site, and it will give you a decent sign of when individuals are visiting it.

WHAT DETERMINES THEIR ONLINE BEHAVIOR?

On the off chance that you investigate activity patterns in light of the times of the week, you may find that you aren't getting great movement on ends of the week when everybody is out, yet you get incredible movement on Friday when individuals are anticipating the end of the week.

You may discover movement spikes at 7 pm around evening time if your specialty is something outside of work, however it may spike at 8 am Monday morning in the event that it is something that is imperative to a workplace. You truly need to get into the psyche of your normal client to figure out how to time your presenting on get the most introduction.

For example, on the off chance that you are attempting to lease a house or room, you can place yourself in individuals' shoes and understand that Thursday and Friday postings in the wake of working hours work best. That is the point at which they are destined to be web based searching for a place to lease and visit throughout the end of the week.

Whatever is left of the week, their psyches are on different things, so why squander your opportunity posting when they're not by any means taking note? Time your postings to when you as of now have their consideration.

Great Ways To Capture Attention

Since you comprehend the mechanics of creating activity back to your site, we should discuss some not all that conspicuous ways that can manufacture fervor and buzz for your backlinks. You can see that by utilizing these procedures, you will get more taps on your connections when you go to break down them.

Why they work is halfway human instinct. Individuals are commonly inquisitive. Whatever you're doing is raising that interest to a more elevated amount.

BE VAGUE

When you go to purchase something, the main thing you search for is abandons. It's solitary human instinct. We would prefer not to feel like we've been taken, and a great many people truly detest tapping on a connection just to arrive on a connection homestead or spam page.

That is the reason you would prefer not to give out excessively data when you include your connection. You need to be clear enough to induce energy and interest, yet insufficient to give them the majority of the subtle elements forthright so they can dissect your offer. Thusly, you will likewise demolish the shock.

Extraordinary compared to other promoting methodologies out there is to abstain from giving out excessively data in your backlinks; you never at any point offer in light of highlights, just on benefits. In this way, in case you're endeavoring to get movement to a book on the best way to plant, you don't include a backlink that says: "Come look at my book on cultivating."

That's an exceptional in that spot. Rather, you offer an advantage and make it somewhat ambiguous, similar to: "I spared hundreds on basic need charges, discover how!" If you've additionally looked into the watchwords and "spared hundreds on basic need bills" was one such expression, and you utilized it as your stay content, you're pulling in consideration from the web crawlers as well!

Features AND PICTURES

Regardless of whether somebody isn't keen on what you are offering, he/she may at present need to take a gander at your post just to perceive what the photo is that you've embedded there alongside your post.

This works awesome on Craigslist and on different destinations that permit pictures, yet don't really present them on see until the point that somebody has really clicked onto your posting. Rather, the individual perusing promotions may see a huge amount of advertisements with nothing extraordinary, yet one that says "pic" by it. Voila

Regardless of whether he/she couldn't care less much for your feature, he's/she will click onto that promotion just to see the shrouded picture. In the event that you match that photo with an eye catching feature, you can make certain you've made a mental trigger that few will have the capacity to leave behind.

Once you have him/her to tap on the general promotion, he's/she's as of now there, so you can wager he/she will at any rate read your post, expanding the odds of getting him/her to tap on the backlink as well.

Polarize Your Online Presence

Another methodology that you can use in connection to pulling individuals from various territories is to deliberately charge your online nearness to make it alluring and engaging your objective statistic.

This is vital to use related to rehearses that draw individuals from different locales, as Facebook and Twitter. All things considered, on long range informal communication locales, the item is you until the point that they get the opportunity to discover more about your business.

Until that point, you're offering your identity until the point when some level of trust is come to and individuals will visit your destinations because of your online nearness on informal communication locales.

CAREFUL PROFILE BUILDING

People on social networking sites tend to want to network with other people of similar interests. This makes these types of sites very valuable to help you find new customers to target in your niche. However, they're not going to search these sites the same way that they use Google to search for a product because the product on a social networking site is a person first.

They are generally known via their social networking profiles and then are harvested off these sites and converted into customers later. This makes the careful and thoughtful building of your social networking profile extremely important to attract the right demographic to you as your friends and followers.

The way to get the right people to connect to you on these sites is to use your profile to list activities and interests that coincide with your marketing niche. If you are a financial planner, for instance, you might want to list some good financial planning books in books you've read.

Maybe you follow a specific financial guru, then list their DVDs. The more descriptive and targeted your profile happens to be, the more likely people of similar interests will want to connect with you online.

POST FREQUENTLY

Once you've got the right profile, you want to post frequently to get people used to visiting it. You can post informational links from other sites, as well as your own copy from your own sites and offerings. When you mix in other people's links with your own, the odds that people will click your links increases too since they won't know which links are promoting your offerings and which are informational ones that you're posting to be helpful.

Some sites will require even more frequent postings, like Twitter. There, it's not unusual to post 140 character tweets 7 to 10 times a day. On blogs, posting daily or every other day works great. Some bloggers, however, even post twice a day. The more you post, the more traffic you will generate.

Get Traffic Through Social Networking

As was mentioned earlier, you want to visit and maintain an online presence on sites with large traffic audiences. Twitter and Facebook have massive audiences, and they can be highly targeted once you know how to set up a profile that attracts only the demographic that you seek. However, you still must learn the intricacies of each site and seek to set them up so that you can literally update your posts in your sleep.

TWITTER

Twitter is called a "microblogging" site because the posts consist of 140-character updates that are called tweets.

Obviously, it doesn't take long to craft a tweet, but it does take skill to do it well. Just tweeting isn't going to generate traffic back to your site if you have no followers. That's why it's important to build an attractive and magnetic profile and then actively seek followers. You can do this by just going out and following others in your market niche.

Many will follow back out of pure courtesy. Even if you only have a few followers, you can still gain massive exposure if your tweet is picked up by someone in your audience and retweeted (reposted) to his/her audience too.

If that keeps going from one person to another, your tweet can go viral and reach millions, even if your group of followers is quite small. It is always better, however, to get as many followers as you can in your target niche to increase exposure.

Twitter presents some interesting dynamics in that it's acceptable to post links to your own offerings, whereas other sites might consider them as spam. They also let you tweet many more times a day than other sites will let you post. This is really great to know so that you can automate tweets using services like SocialOomph to schedule tweets at different times of the day, even if they're the same tweet text.

FACEBOOK

Facebook also lets you put in a status update with links, images, videos, etc, but if you post as frequently as you do on Twitter, you'll more than likely lose friends. Tone down the commercial tones for Facebook. The key to all of these sites is to participate and not just post.

You want to give as much as you get, and vote "like" for different people's links and comments so that they will do the same for yours. When they do that, more people will see your content than just your immediate circle of friends due to a sharing feature within Facebook.

Other High Traffic Sites To Mine

Social networks aren't the only places you can add backlinks and comments to get people to come back to your own website. There are many other such places all across the Web, and they all have their pros and cons. Let's take a look at a few other places to concentrate on posting backlinks back to your website.

POPULAR NICHE BLOGS

If you don't know what high-traffic blogs are out there in your niche, take a look at Technorati.com. They list all manners of blogs out there and can give you some idea of their popularity. All you have to do is to locate a few within your market niche and then go out and visit them online.

Read a few of their posts and then post a comment. Many blogs will allow you to post a link back to your own website if you are participating and contributing to the conversation. If you are just self-promoting, your link will not be posted, and you may get banned from that audience too as a spammer.

ONLINE DISCUSSION GROUPS

There are groups within Yahoo and also within Google. Even Facebook supports groups that meet to discuss a specific topic of interest to its participants. When you have a number of people all looking for information within your market niche, it makes it the perfect place to go, establish an online presence, and make yourself the expert there.

More people will follow you back, particularly if you are allowed to post your backlinks as part of an automatic signature line that gets added to every post you answer within that group.

ARTICLE DIRECTORIES

Article catalogs pull in a wide range of individuals who may not be on different destinations around the Web. They are exceedingly ordered by the web indexes as well. It's a simple thing to post a couple of articles inside your specialty in these article registries and utilize the asset box to set up joins back to your online exercises somewhere else.

For whatever length of time that you are following the terms of administration with respect to your connections, you can utilize them to help advance distinctive zones on the Web where you are working together.

You will be unable to put a connection straightforwardly to an item deals page, as a few locales won't permit this, yet you can absolutely drive activity back to a page on your site that is more educational and that additionally has interfaces back to your items.

Utilize catchphrases in your articles to make these web search tool agreeable and additionally human neighborly, and you will have better outcomes with article showcasing to make more activity for your connections.

Paying For Traffic

Ultimately, we need to examine the likelihood of paying for movement. The past procedures that were examined are known as "natural" approaches to produce movement; notwithstanding, you can pick a more straightforward way and just pay to get activity.

We don't prescribe that you pay for the activity itself, as this won't be focused on and can truly execute your Google standing. Rather, look to utilize promoting stages to pay others to construct movement streams back to your site by paying for powerful backlink creation and publicizing presentation without really paying for hits to your site. This is finished by setting up publicizing efforts, partner projects, or referral motivations.

Promoting CAMPAIGNS

We as of now discussed Social Ads from Facebook that can be utilized to produce movement back to your site. Google AdWords battles is a compensation for each snap organize that offers great presentation in light of the catchphrases that you select, and you set your estimating by and large. Other web indexes likewise have their own publicizing stages that can be set up to make a crusade where you purchase activity for your merchandise and ventures on the web.

AFFILIATE PROGRAMS

Offshoot programs incorporate Google AdSense, where distributers get paid to publicize the contributions in Google AdWords crusades. Nonetheless, there are different systems that offer subsidiary projects for different kinds of advertising that compensation on a commission structure for an offer of an item or for an activity played out that creates a potential customer at times.

Investigate setting up your very own member program to make movement back to your site on any number of partner systems, including JVZoo.com, Commission Junction (CJ.com) or ClickBank.com. It very well may be exceptionally costly to join as a shipper, yet it's justified, despite all the trouble to produce deals and also movement back to your site.

REFERRAL INCENTIVES

On the off chance that you are the main individual setting up joins back to your site, it will take a ton longer than if you can convince others to begin doing it for you. One approach to do that is through referral motivating forces.

On the off chance that somebody realizes that in the event that he/she alludes somebody to your site, the referral joins, and that individual makes a simple $10, he/she will be more spurred to do that for you. You will need to confine the payouts to clients who join, as well as satisfy some promoting action that causes you to take care of the expense of the referral motivating force as well.

A few spots will give out referral motivators for individuals who allude a client who joins with an arrangement and remains with it for a set timeframe. Some are multi-layered where you get a commission off of your referrals and their referrals as well if individuals purchase something.

There are various approaches to set up viable referral motivations, so you have an entire armed force of individuals willing to go out and post backlinks for you. The decent thing is that you don't pay them except if they convey back business to your entryway.

About The Author

JAMAL ABUKOU
PMP, MPM®, CIPM®, CPRM™, SCMS-A, SCDM-A, SFC, SSYB, SSGB

Is a proactive and highly diligent chartered civil engineer, *PMP, MPM®, CIPM®, CPRM™, SCMS-A, SCDM-A, SFC, SSYB, SSGB* Certified with 30+ years of experience in Strategic Program and Project Management, Planning, Business Development and Environmental Management Strategies.

Learn more about Jamal at
http://abukou.wix.com/jamalabukou

Follow Jamal on LinkedIn at
ae.linkedin.com/in/JamalAbukouStrategicPPMO

Follow Jamal on Amazon at
https://www.amazon.com/author/jamalabukou

Follow Jamal on Facebook at

http://www.facebook.com/jamal.abukou

Follow Jamal on Twitter at

http://twitter.com/AbukouJamal

Follow Jamal on Google+ at

https://plus.google.com/106682869475993881190/about/p/pub

Selective Books By The Author

To view the Full List of Books by the author, please visit the following link:

amazon.com/author/jamalabukou

You will find valuable books in various topics such as:

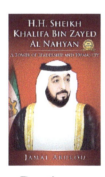

eBook: A Tower Of Leadership And Humanity

Paperback: A Tower Of Leadership And Humanity

eBook: Money Finder's Wikipedia

Paperback: Money Finder's Wikipedia

Kindle eBook: Internet Marketing Wikipedia

Paperback: Internet Marketing Wikipedia

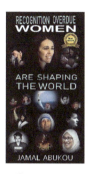

eBook: Women Are Shaping The World

Paperback: Women Are Shaping The World

eBook: How To Drive Unlimited Traffic To Your Website

Paperback: How To Drive Unlimited Traffic To Your Website

eBook: Strategic Project Management. Your Whole Life Is Full Of Projects That Need To Be Managed Wisely

Paperback: Strategic Project Management

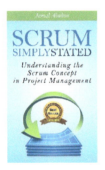

eBook: SCRUM Simply Stated. The Latest, Most Advanced Project Management Method

Paperback: SCRUM Simply Stated

eBook: The Online Marketing Blueprint

Paperback: The Online Marketing Blueprint

eBook: How To Skyrocket Your Sales

Paperback: How To Skyrocket Your Sales

eBook: How to Make Passive Income

Paperback: How to Make Passive Income

eBook: Copywriter's Wikipedia: Easy Money In A Week

Paperback: Copywriter's Wikipedia

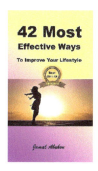

eBook: [42 Most Effective Ways To Improve Your Lifestyle](#)

Paperback: [42 Most Effective Ways To Improve Your Lifestyle](#)

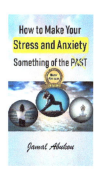

eBook: [How to Make Your Stress and Anxiety Something of the PAST](#)

Paperback: [How to Make Your Stress and Anxiety Something of the PAST](#)

Paperback: Coloring Book Skill Challenge: Dare Your Skills To The LIMIT

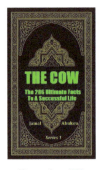

eBook: The 286 Ultimate Facts To A Successful Life

Paperback: The 286 Ultimate Facts To A Successful Life

One Last Thing...

If you enjoyed this book or found it useful, I would be very grateful if you would post a short review on Amazon. Your support really does make a difference and I read all the reviews personally so I can get your feedback and make this book even better.

If you would like to leave a review, then all you need to do is click the review link on this book's page on Amazon here:

http://www.amazon.com/dp/B00QIMWXM2

Thanks again for your support!